Knitting Socks
Quick and Easy Way to Master Sock Knitting

Copyright © 2020

DEDICATION

Contents

Sock knitting is hugely popular for a variety of reasons. Sock projects are much more portable than sweaters, they're ideal for gifting, and there are so many wonderful, beautiful, and fun yarns for knitted socks. And it's not as difficult as it might seem, really! Knitting socks is very straightforward, making them great projects for travel, or knitting at the game or while waiting for the kids to finish their sports practice. As long as you've got the right number of stitches and pay attention to the instructions, it will all work out.

One of the wonderful things about sock knitting is that it can be as simple or as challenging as you like. Once you've mastered a standard pattern, you make it over and over again. I find knitting plain socks with fun yarns very relaxing. Or if you're up for a challenge, there are all sorts of patterns and variations. Sock knitters all have their preferences: which needles to use, which yarn they prefer, the construction they find easiest, which heel and toe variations fit them best. Once you've tried your first sock pattern, you'll be well equipped to try others and form your own opinions!

Happy sock knitting!

How to Knit Socks: Basic Recipe

Materials:

- Superwash wool of any weight
- Knitter's Pride Marblz, Zing, or Symfonie Dreamz DPNs in the corresponding size
- Tapestry needle

Step 1: ESTABLISH GAUGE

No matter what yarn you're working with, or size sock — from baby to grown man — you're knitting the basic model for making on is GENERALLY the same. The difference is really only in the numbers. To that end, you'll first need to knit a swatch with chosen yarn, needles, and stitch pattern to establish stitch and row gauge. You'll need this info for the next step.

For the purposes of this tutorial, let's say we're using size U.S. 6/4 mm needles and sport-weight yarn, when knit in Stockinette Stitch, gives us a gauge of **4 stitches and 6 1/2 rows per inch.**

Step 2: CALCULATE CAST ON (CO) NUMBER

To get started, you have a couple of choices: either measure the foot circumference of the person you're going to knit for or use the average sizing provided by Yarn Standards. I prefer the latter.

Man Shoe Size Chart

(U.S. Sizes)		6-8½	9-11½	12-14
11a.	Foot Circum. (in.)	8	9	10
	(cm.)	20.5	23	25.5
11b.	Sock Height	7½	8	8½
		19	20.5	21.5
11c.	Total Foot Length	9¼-10	10¼-11	11¼-12
		23.5-25	26-28	28.5-30.5

Since the genesis of this post was the WWII patriotic knitting for soldiers effort, let's go with the numbers correlating to a men's medium size sock for our pattern. To calculate a cast on number, you'll just need to multiply the foot circumference and stitch gauge numbers. Using our results from Step 1, and the chart above that will look like this:

9 in. x 4 sts = 36

That's it! Keeping in mind that we may need to adjust the number one way or another to accommodate a stitch pattern, we know that 36 stitches is a good amount to cast on for our socks! Bonus: If we want to work in 2×2 ribbing, we'll need a multiple of 4. If we want to work in 1×1 ribbing, we'll need a multiple of 2. Either way, 36 means we're golden. High-five!

Step 3: THE LEG

CO stitches to dpns (double-pointed needles). Divide evenly between needles; join, taking care not to twist.

Knit stitches in desired stitch pattern, maybe ribbed for a cuff, then stockinette for the leg, rib for the whole let, seed stitch; you do you! The length is really a preference; ankle, calf, or knee-high are all worked the same except for how long. Using the chart and our calculations, however, our numbers will look like this:

$$8 \text{ in (height)} \times 6\ 1/2 \text{ rows} = 52$$

This means we'll work 52 rounds of leg stitches in our desired stitch pattern.

Step 4: THE HEEL FLAP (Square heel method)

The heel flap is the only part of this sock that won't be knit in-the-round. For this step, you'll place half (the front/instep) stitches on waste yarn or spare needles, and the other half (the heel) on 1 needle. For our example, that means **18 heel stitches**. I like a thick heel, so recommend knitting in the following manner, but you can technically use any stitch pattern that makes you happy.

Row 1: *Slip (Sl)1, knit (k) 1; repeat from * to end.

Row 2: Sl 1, purl (p) to end.

Repeat those two rows until your heel flap is a square. If math makes your whole hear sing, then, by all means, do the multiplication to determine exactly how many rows that will be. If not though, do what I do, which is to just fold the heel from corner to corner. Once it's even, you'll know you have a square and your heel is complete!

Step 5: TURNING THE HEEL

Since we're not two-dimensional beings (no offense to Flat Stanley), we need some shaping to cup our heel. This is created with a series of simple, short rows. Here's how:

To turn a heel, you're going work 2/3 of the RIGHT SIDE heel stitches, decrease, and turn. Then you'll work 1/3 of the WRONG SIDE heel flap, decrease and turn, work to gap, decrease and turn, etc. For our example using 18 heel stitches, that looks like this:

Row 1: Sl 1, k11, ssk (slip, slip, knit together through the back loop). Turn.

Row 2: Sl 1, p5, p2tog. Turn.

Row 3: Sl 1, k to 1 st before gap, ssk. Turn.

Row 4: Sl 1, p to 1 st before gap, p2tog. Turn.

Repeat Rows 3-4 until all heel stitches are worked.

Step 6: THE GUSSET

For this part of the sock, you'll revert to working in rounds.

Rnd 1: Place half of the heel stitches on free dpn (Needle 1), with the same dpn pick up stitches evenly along the first side of heel; place instep stitches on Needle 2; use Needle 3 to pick up stitches along the second side of heel and work remaining heel stitches.

Rnd 2: Work in straight pattern stitch. (i.e. Knit all stitches, if working in Stockinette Stitch)

Rnd 3: Needle 1, work to last 3 sts, k2tog, k1; Needle 2, work straight (i.e. knit); Needle 3, k1, ssk, work to end.

Rnd 4: Work in straight pattern stitch.

Repeat Rnds 3-4 until you get back to your original, CO number of stitches. For our purposes, that would be **36 sts.**

Step 7: THE FOOT

Work every round in straight pattern stitch until foot is 2 1/2"
shorter than the desired length. Using the chart above, we want our

foot to be 11", so that means we'll work rounds until the foot measures 8 1/2".

Step 8: THE TOE

Arrange stitches so 1/2 (top) are on Needle 2, and 1/4 are on Needles 1 & 3. For us that means, Needles 1 & 3 have 9 stitches each, and Needle 1 has 18. Shape as follows:

Rnd 1: Needle 1, k to last 3 sts, k2 tog, k1; Needle 2, k1, ssk, k to last 3 sts, k2tog, k1; Needle 3, k1, ssk, k to end.

Rnd 2: Knit. (I'm making the assumption here that regardless of foot stitch pattern that the stitcher will work the toe in Stockinette as is necessary for the next step to look right.)

Repeat Rnds 1-2 until about 1/3 of the stitches, rounded to an even number, remain. For us, let's say 12 sts.

Cut yarn, leaving a long tail for grafting.

Step 9: GRAFTING TOE

We'll seamlessly graft stitches together using Kitchener Stitch. To do so, you'll need to divide the stitches evenly over 2 needles and hold parallel. Thread tail into tapestry needle and work as follows:

Set up:

- Insert tapestry needle purlwise into the first stitch on FRONT needle. Pull tail through, but don't let the stitch fall off.

- Insert tapestry needle knitwise into the first stitch on the BACK needle. Pull tail through, but don't let the stitch fall off.

Begin Grafting:

- Insert tapestry needle knitwise into the first stitch on the FRONT needle and pull tail through, letting it fall off the knitting needle;

- Insert tapestry needle purlwise into the next stitch on the FRONT needle and pull the tail through, WITHOUT letting the stitch fall off knitting needle.

- Insert tapestry needle purlwise into the first stitch on the BACK needle and pull tail through, letting it fall off the knitting needle;

- Insert tapestry needle knitwise into the next stitch on the FRONT needle and pull the tail through, WITHOUT letting the stitch fall off knitting needle.

Repeat those 4 steps until all stitches are grafted. Weave in ends.

Knit a Small Sock With a Step-By-Step Practice Pattern

What you'll need

Equipment / Tools

- 1 Pair of scissors

- 1 Yarn needle

- 1 Ruler or tape measure

- 1 Size-7 US double-pointed needles (set of 4)

Materials

- 1 Scrap of worsted weight yarn, about 20 yards

Instructions

Cast on and Join in Round

To begin, cast on 20 stitches onto one needle.

- Distribute the stitches onto three of the four needles.

- Slide the stitches to the end of the needle, beginning with the first cast on stitch.

- Slip 7 stitches one at a time onto another needle.

- Slip the next 6 stitches onto a third needle.

Once the stitches are evenly distributed, join the work in the round.

- Slip the first cast on stitch onto the needle with the last cast on stitch.

- Slip the last stitch over the first stitch and onto the last needle.

At this point, you can slip a stitch holder onto the needle to mark the end of the row. Or, you can note where the tail from your cast on is; this is the end of the row.

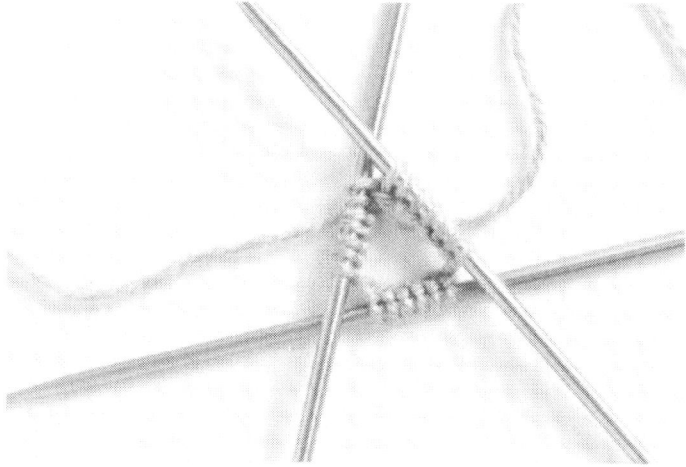

Knit the Ribbing

Work in knit 1, purl 1 ribbing for 4 rounds.

Use the fourth needle to work across the stitches on one needle. After that needle is empty, use it to work across the next needle, and so on.

If you're new to double-pointed needles, you might need to knit a little slower than usual. Once you've knit a couple of rounds, the work will begin to flow and feel much more stable.

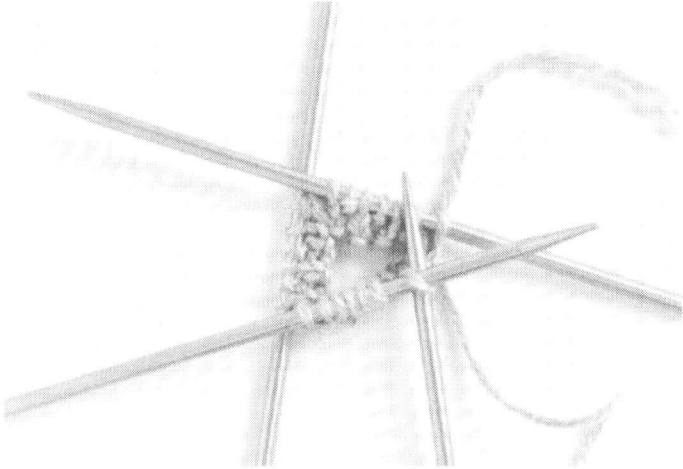

Knit the Leg

Knit every round for one inch. When knitting in the round, knitting every row produces stockinette stitch.

The leg is the part of the sock that often has interesting stitch patterns or cables worked into it. But when you're first learning, simple stockinette makes it easier to get started.

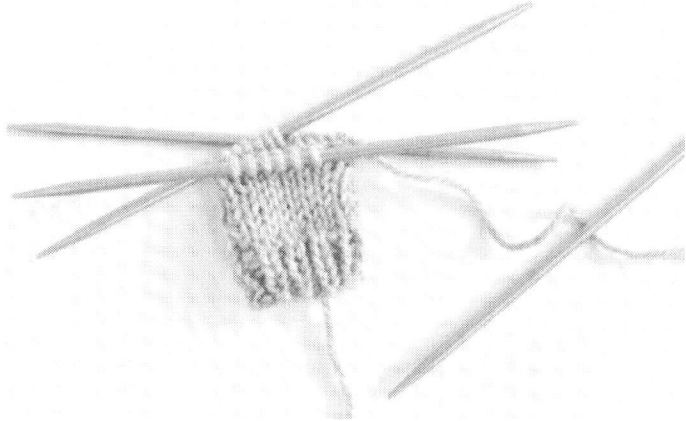

Knit the Heel Flap

There are different methods for knitting a heel, but one of the most common is using a heel flap and then "turning the heel."

- Knit the first 10 stitches of the round onto one needle.
- To make it easier to work with, slip the other 10 stitches onto one needle and allow them to hang while you work on the other stitches.

Knit the heel flap with a two-row repeat:

- **Row 1 (wrong side):** Slip the first stitch purlwise with the yarn in front, purl the rest of the stitches.

- **Row 2:** Slip the first stitch purlwise with the yarn in back, knit the rest of the stitches.

- Repeat these two rows 4 more times, until you've worked 10 rows total, ending on the knit side.

Turn the Heel

Turning the heel is a common method for making the cup your heel sit in when you wear the sock. This method uses short rows, turning the work and knitting back over the stitches you just worked without knitting across the whole row.

As before, slip the stitches purlwise with the yarn in front.

- **Row 1:** Slip 1, purl 5, purl 2 together, purl one. Turn the work, leaving one stitch unworked.

- **Row 2:** Slip 1, knit 3, slip, slip, knit (SSK), knit 1. Turn the work, leaving one stitch unworked.

- **Row 3:** Slip 1, purl 4, purl 2 together. Turn the work. There are no unworked stitches.

- **Row 4:** Slip 1, knit 4, SSK. There are no unworked stitches. Six stitches remain on the needle.

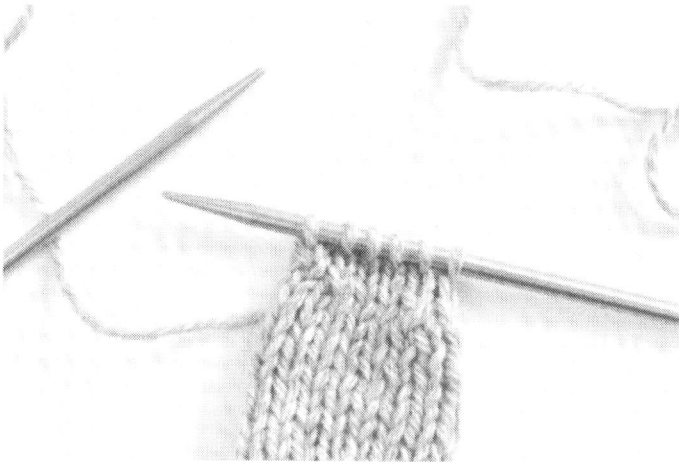

Pick Up Stitches and Divide Them Again

The gusset of a sock knits the leg stitches and the heel stitches back together. It shapes the sock so it fits around the heel and the top of the foot.

- Take an empty needle and pick up and knit six stitches along the side of the heel flap. The stitches should be easy to find because they are the slipped stitches along the edge of the heel flap.

- Use another needle to knit across the 10 stitches of the leg you left unworked as you made the heel flap.

- Use the newly empty needle to pick up and knit six stitches along the second side of the heel flap. Knit three of the stitches from the heel itself.

- Slip the last three stitches of the heel onto the needle with the first stitches you picked up. Use the newly empty needle and knit the three slipped stitches, along with the first stitches you picked up.

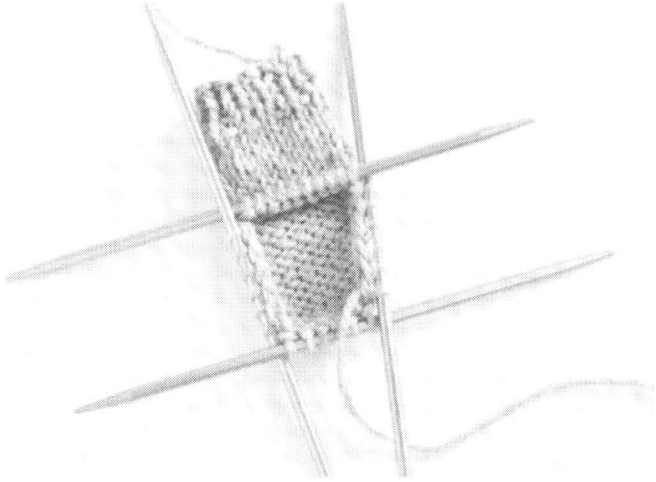

Work the Gusset

The stitches from the leg are on needle one, the next needle is needle 2, and the needle you just finished knitting is needle 3.

Now it's time to shape the gusset.

- **Row 1:** Knit across the first needle. On the second needle, knit 1, SSK, and knit to the end of the needle. On the third needle, knit to within 3 stitches of the end of the row, knit two together, and knit the last stitch.

- **Row 2:** Knit every stitch.

- Repeat these two rows until you have five stitches on each of the second and third needles; 20 stitches total.

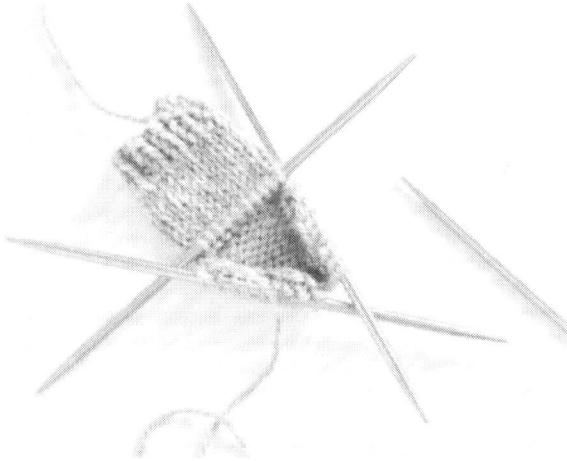

Knit the Foot

Once you have the gusset shaped and are back to 20 stitches, knit every stitch in every round for another inch. This makes the foot part of the sock.

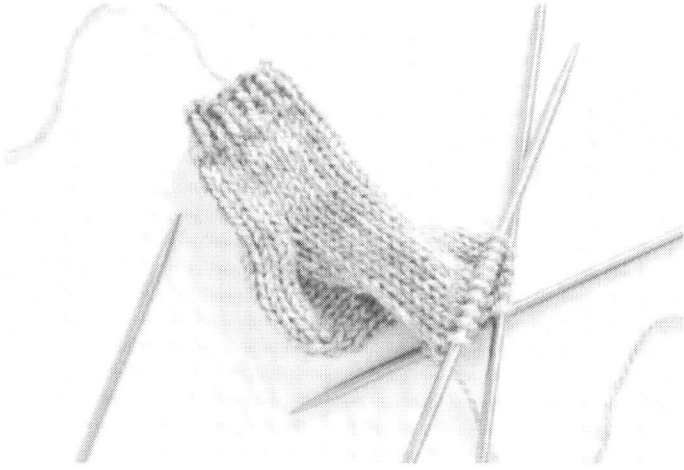

Knit the Sock Toe

Now shape the toe of the sock. As before, the stitches on the top of the sock are on needle one, followed by needle two and needle three.

- **Row 1:** On needle one, knit 1, SSK to the last three stitches, knit 2 together, knit 1. On needle two, knit 1, SSK, and knit to the end. On needle three, knit to the last three stitches, knit 2 together, knit 1.

- **Row 2:** Knit every stitch.

- **Row 3:** Repeat row 1. You will have 12 stitches remaining.

- Slip the stitches from needle two onto needle three so that you have two needles with 6 stitches each.

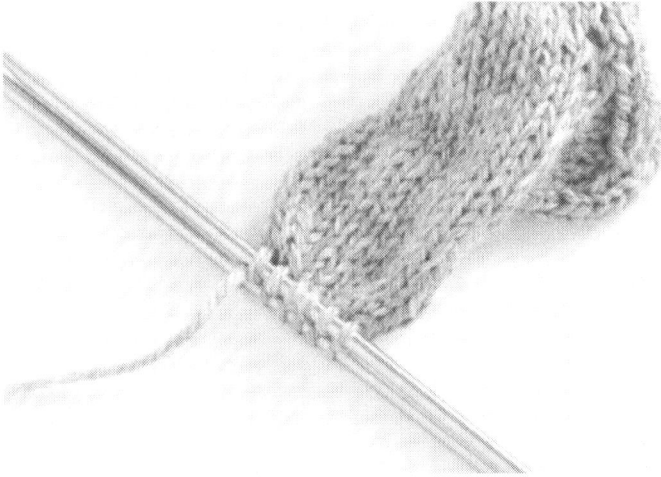

Finish the Sock

To finish the sock, practice the standard way of closing off a sock, known as grafting or the Kitchener stitch. Weave in the ends.

Knit Two Socks on Two Circular Needles

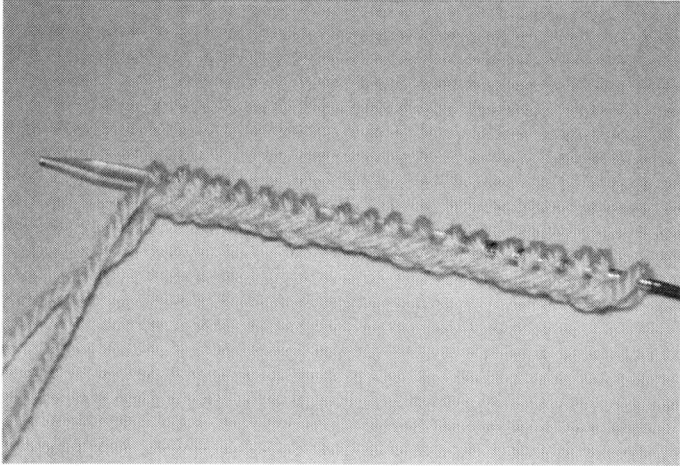

Abbreviations

- k = knit

- k2tog = knit two sts together as one

- p = purl

- rep = repeat

- rnd(s) = round(s)

- RS = right side; the public side of the work

- sl = slip

- ssk = slip, slip, knit two slipped sts together through the back loop

- st(s) = stitch(es)

- WS = wrong side; the inside of the work

Notes

- When selecting the two circular needles, try to find two that are different in some way. They can be different materials, colors, or lengths; just something if that makes it easier for you to tell them apart.

- Start with your yarn wound into two balls; each sock will be knit with its own ball of yarn. Since you're just practicing, you might even want to make the socks in two different colors to remind you to switch balls when you change which sock you're working.

What you'll need

Equipment / Tools

- 2 16 to 24-inch circular needles in size appropriate for the yarn

- stitch marker or safety pin

- Yarn or tapestry needle

- Scissors

Materials

- 40 yard worsted weight smooth yarn in light or bright color, wound in two separate balls

Instructions

Sock 1: Cast On

- When knitting two socks at a time on two circular needles, you don't knit all of Sock 1 and then all of Sock 2. You knit the first half of Sock 1, then the first half of Sock 2; these stitches will conveniently be on the same needle. Then you switch to the other needle to knit the second half of Sock 2, followed by the second half of Sock 2. To begin, all the stitches of the first sock are cast on at once.

- With needle A (clear tips) and yarn ball A, cast on 20 stitches.

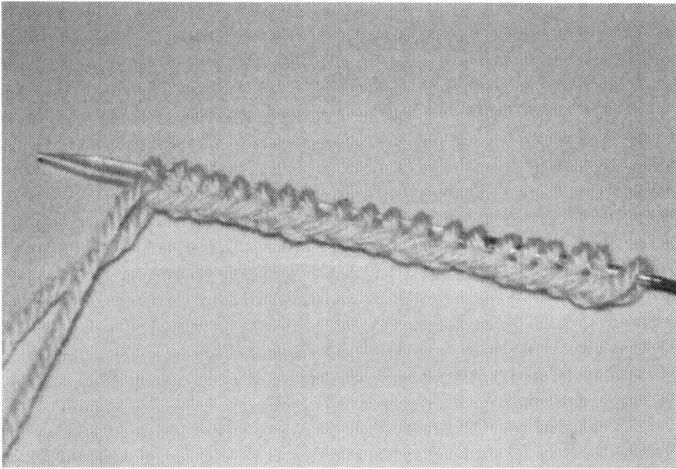

Sock 1: Join in the Round

Slip 10 stitches from needle A to needle B (silver tips). Move the stitches from the needle tips they're currently on to the other end. Now you need to join your stitches into a round so that you can knit them like a tube.

Tip

If your needles aren't the same length, be careful not to slide
the stitches off the shorter needle.

Thread the yarn tail from the cast-on on a yarn needle; insert the
needle the yarn through the first stitch on the opposite side from
where the tail is. The first sock is cast on and ready to knit.

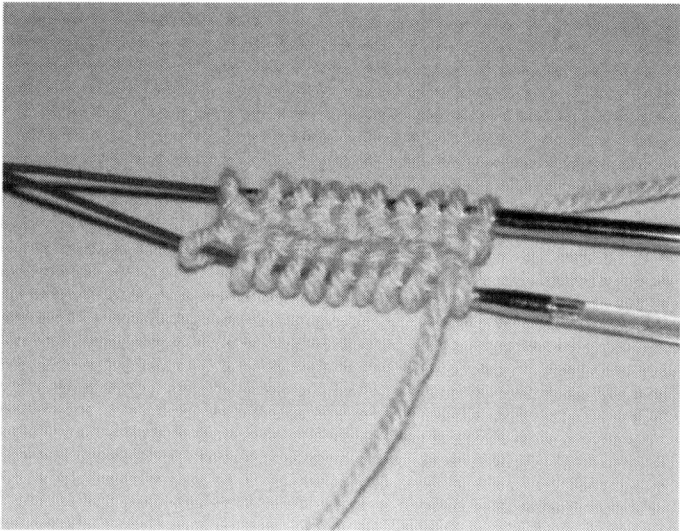

Sock 2: Cast On and Join

Slide the stitches of the first sock back onto the cables of the needles so they're out of the way and in no danger of falling off while you set up the second sock.

- With needle A and yarn ball B, cast on 20 stitches. Put half the stitches on needle B and join in the round as before.

There are now two socks on two needles, A (clear tips) and B (silver tips), with half of the stitches for each sock on each one of the needles.

Tip

Mark which sock is the first sock. Place other markers to indicate the ends of the round. While this isn't as crucial if you're using needles that don't match, it is always helpful to have reminders of where you are in circular knitting.

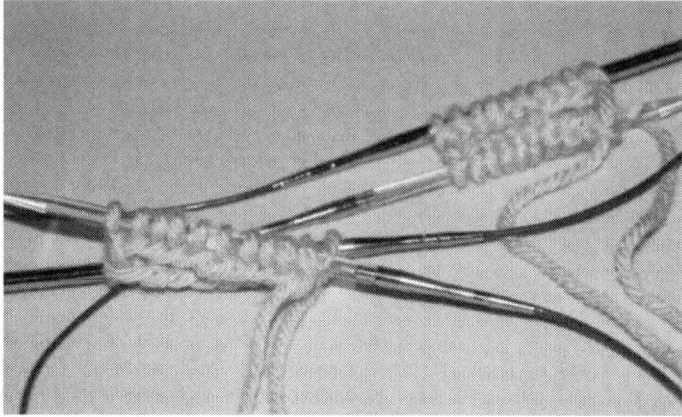

First Half of Sock 1

Turn the needles so you can knit the stitches from the first half of the first sock: the needle A tip holding the first half of the sock should be in your left hand. Take the other end of needle A in your right hand.

- Using the two ends of needle A, and the attached working yarn from yarn ball A, knit the stitches from the first half of Sock 1 from one end to the other end.

If this were an actual sock, you'd probably work ribbing here; for this sample sock tutorial, knit across all 10 stitches.

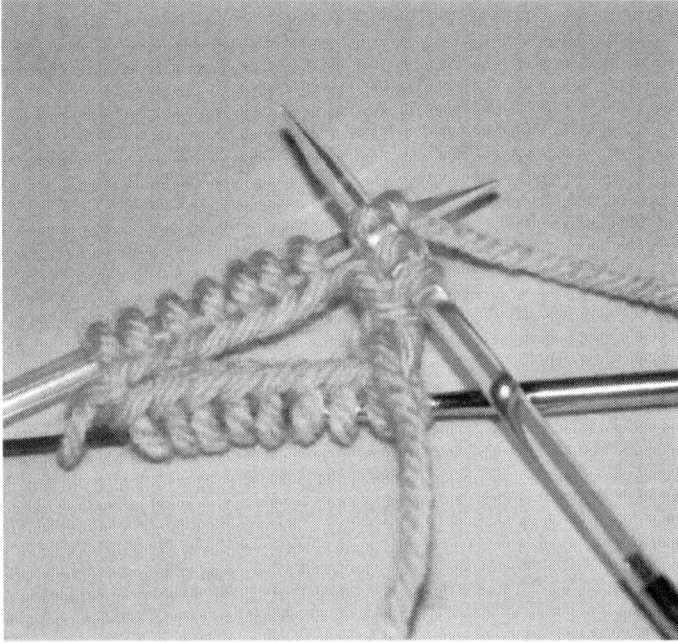

First Half of Sock 2

The first half of Sock 2 is also on needle A. Slide the stitches of the first half of Sock 1 down onto the cables to keep them out of the way.

- Continue using the two ends of needle A, but the attached working yarn from yarn ball B, knit the stitches from the first half of the Sock 2 from one end to the other end.

Remember: you're working with two ends of needle A, and the ball of yarn attached to Sock 2, not the one used for Sock 1.

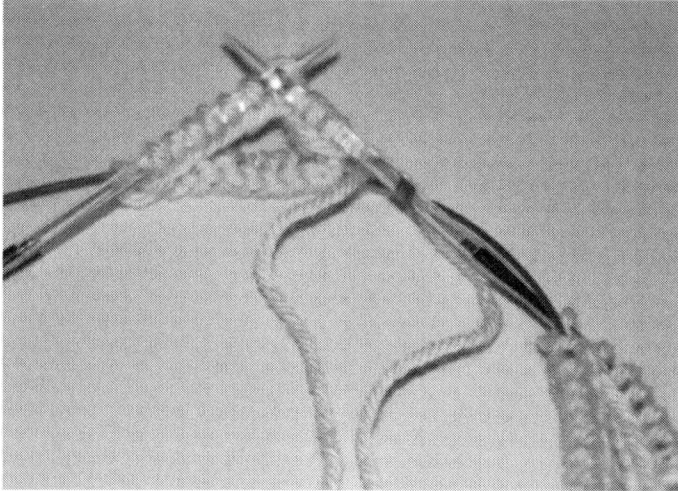

Finishing the First Round

For the second half of the round, you are switching from needle A to B. This time you begin with the Sock 2. Flip the work around so you have access to Needle B and its stitches.

- Push the stitches of the second half of Sock 2 up on the end of needle B; using the other end of needle B and yarn ball B, knit 10 stitches.

Slide the stitches of Sock 2 onto the cable so they are out of the way. The second half of Sock 1 is also on needle B.

- Continuing with the two ends of needle B but the yarn from yarn ball A, knit 10 stitches from the second half of Sock 1 from one end to the other.

You've now finished one round of knitting on two socks at once.

The Legs

- Continue in working around as above, working in order and using needle A for the first halves and needle B for the second halves: first half of Sock 1, first half of Sock 2, second half of Sock 2, second half of Sock 1.

- Work in stockinette stitch (knit all rounds) for the leg portion of your practice sock, until you're nice and comfortable with the process—approximately 2 inches.

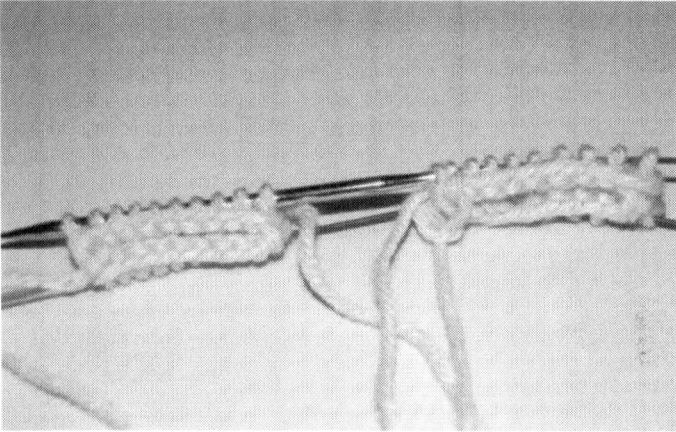

Heel Flaps

With the sock legs the specified (or desired) length, it's time to work the heel. Heel flaps are worked flat back and forth on half the stitches of a sock. This means you'll be working back and forth on just one needle (B) too, while the other half of the stitches rest on the other needle (A). The heels of the sample sock are worked in garter stitch.

- **Next row**: for Sock 1, sl1 pwise, k10 sts; for Sock 2, sl1 pwise, k10 sts.

Repeat this row until 10 rows have been worked; end on a right side

37

row.

Turning the Heels and First Gusset

To turn a heel, you have to work short rows. This means you aren't working across all the stitches of a single sock's heel on every row. When you're working socks two at a time, it's easiest to complete one heel turn before starting the other.

- **Row 1**: sl1, k5, k2tog, k1, turn.
- **Row 2**: sl1, k3, ssk, k1, turn.

- **Row 3**: sl1, k4, k2tog, turn.
- **Row 4**: sl1, k4, ssk.

Once the heel has been worked, pick up and knit gusset stitches along the left side of the first sock's heel flap, 1 st in each slipped stitch.

Adjust the needles as necessary to do the same thing on the second sock. Leave the second half of the heel flap for now.

Second Gusset

To get the yarn in position for picking up the remaining stitches along the other sides of the heel flaps, it's time to reactivate needle A.

- **Next first half**: using needle A and yarn ball A, knit from the last picked-up stitch of the left gusset on Sock 1 across the 10 instep stitches; continuing with needle A and yarn ball B, knit from the last picked-up stitch of the left gusset on Sock 2 across the 10 instep stitches.

- **Next second half**: using needle B and continuing with yarn ball B, pick up 1 stitch in each slipped stitch along the right side of the Sock 2's heel flap, then knit across remaining heel and gusset stitches of Sock 2; continuing with needle B and yarn ball A, pick up 1 stitch in each slipped stitch along the right side of the Sock 1's heel flap, then knit across remaining heel and gusset stitches of Sock 1.

Traditionally the center back of the heel is considered the beginning of the round once the heel turn has been worked, but here it's the end of this needle. Once you understand the movement of the stitches around the needles, adjust to fit your preferences.

Gusset Decreases and Foot

The gusset stitches are now decreased away until the original number of stitches has been restored. Remember that the stitches that are decreased are all on that first needle; the stitches that weren't part of the heel are worked even.

Tip

If you had been working a pattern stitch on the leg of your sock that continued on the foot, you would continue to work it only on the stitches on the second needle.

- **Decrease rnd, first half**: using needle A, yarn ball A, and working on Sock 1, k1, k2tog, knit to last 3 sts from the end of the first half of the sock, ssk, k1; using needle A, yarn ball B, and working on Sock 2, k1, k2tog, knit to last 3 sts from the end of the first part of the sock, ssk, k1.

- **Decrease rnd, second half**: using needle B, knit.

- **Next rnd**: using appropriate needle, knit.

Repeat last two rounds until there are 20 stitches remaining in each sock.

Work even, without decreasing for about seven rnds, or about 1 inch for the sample sock.

Shape Toe

On the first half of the sample sock,

- **Decrease rnd, first half**: using needle A, yarn ball A, and working on Sock 1, k1, k2tog, knit to 3 stitches from end, ssk, k1; using needle A, yarn ball B, and working on Sock 2, k1, k2tog, knit to 3 stitches from end, ssk, k1.

- **Decrease rnd, second half**: using needle B, yarn ball B, and working on Sock 2, k1, k2tog, knit to 3 stitches from end, ssk, k1; using needle B, yarn ball A, and working on Sock 1, k1, k2tog, knit to 3 stitches from end, ssk, k1;

- **Next rnd**: using appropriate needle, knit.

Repeat these two rounds until 12 stitches remain.

Finishing

If you were knitting socks that were meant to be worn by a person, you would probably want to graft the toes closed one at a time in the same way that you would if you were knitting a single sock at a time.

For the demonstration socks, simply cut the working yarn, threaded it onto a yarn needle and fasten off the remaining stitches as you would to close a hat.

Pull tight and you've just finished two socks at once.

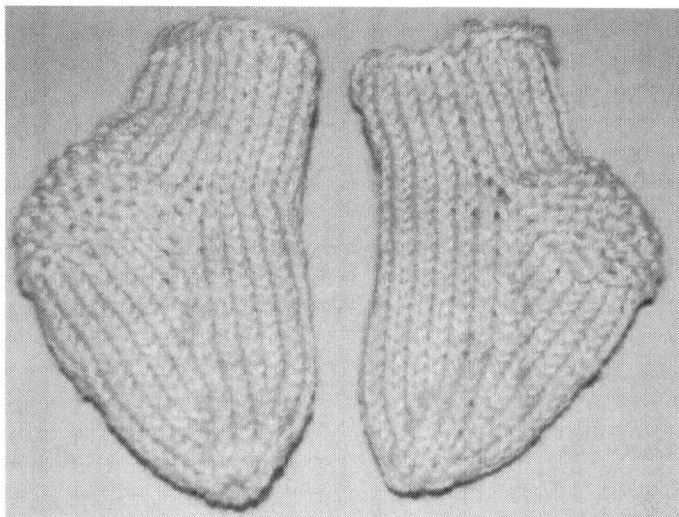

Knit Simple Toddler Socks

Sizing / Finished Measurements

- The larger size is shown in the photo.

- Sizes: 1-3 (4-5) year old foot

- Leg Circumference: 4-3/4 (5-1/4) inches

- Foot Circumference: 5 (5-1/2) inches
- Foot Length: 5 (6) inches

Gauge

34 stitches and 44 rounds = 4 inches in Stockinette stitch in the round

Abbreviations

- k = knit
- k2tog = knit 2 sts together
- p = purl
- p2tog = purl 2 sts together
- RS = right side; the side of the fabric facing out
- rep = repeat
- rnd(s) = round(s)
- sl = slip; to transfer st(s) from needle to needle without turning or working it
- ssk = slip 1 st as if to knit, slip 2nd st as if to knit, insert left

needle from left to right and to front of both sts, knit them together through the back loops

- st(s) = stitch(es)
- WS = wrong side; the side of the fabric facing in
- [ ] = repeat instructions within brackets as directed

2x2 Rib in the Round (multiple of 4 sts)

All rnds: *k2, p2; rep from * to end of rnd.

Notes

Instructions are given for the smaller size first with the larger size in parentheses. Where only one instruction is given it applies to both sizes.

What you'll need:

Equipment / Tools

- US 1 (2.25 mm) double-pointed knitting needles
- Yarn or tapestry needle

- Scissors

Materials

- 130 to 145 yard fingering weight yarn

Instructions

Cuff and Leg

Cast on 40 (44) stitches. Divide sts evenly onto three needles and join for working in the round, placing marker for beginning of round. Work in 2x2 Rib for 1 inch. Continue in Stockinette stitch (knit every stitch in every round) until piece measures 2 1/2 (3) inches.

Heel Flap

With instep stitches on hold, work heel on 20 (22) stitches back and forth in rows. Redistribute stitches on set up rnd.

Setup rnd: with needle 1, k10 (11); with needle 2, k10 (11); with needle 3, k10 (11); slip remaining sts of rnd onto the right end of needle 1—20 (22) sts on needle 1.

The stitches on needles 2 and 3 are on hold. Continue working flat back and forth with needle 1 and an empty needle as follows:

- **Row 1:** *sl1, k1; rep from * to end.
- **Row 2:** sl1, purl to end.

Rep rows 1 and 2 19 (21) more times, or until heel flap is roughly square, ending with a WS row.

Tip

> The slipped-stitch pattern used on the heel provides a denser fabric at a place where socks get a lot of wear. The slipped stitches on the first and last stitches create a chain selvage that is easier to see when you go to pick up stitches in it later, when you make the gusset.

Turn the Heel

Continue in rows to turn the heel, changing the direction of the fabric. Review common knitting decreases like kt2tog and ssk if necessary.

- **Row 1 (RS):** sl1, k10 (12), ssk, k1, turn work.
- **Row 2 (WS):** sl1, p5, p2tog, p1, turn work.
- **Row 3:** sl1, k6, ssk, k1, turn.

- **Row 4**: sl1, p7, p2tog, p1, turn.

- **Row 5**: sl1, k8, ssk, k1, turn.

- **Row 6**: sl1, p9, p2tog, p1, turn.

- **Row 7**: sl1, k10, ssk, k1, turn.

Larger Size Only

- **Row 8**: slip 1, p11, p2tog, p1, turn.

- **Row 9**: knit.

Gusset

For the gusset you will be picking up and knitting the slipped stitches of the chain selvage along each side of the heel flap.

Redistribute sts: the left half of heel flap stay on needle 1, the right half left are placed on the end of needle 3. The working yarn is at the left end of needle 1.

Next rnd: with needle 1, pick up and knit 10 (11) sts from side of heel flap; with new needle 2, k20 (22) instep sts; with new needle 3, pick up and knit 10 (11) sts from side of heel flap, k10 (11) of other half of heel flap.

The center of the bottom of the foot is now at the beginning of the round. Place marker for beginning/end of rnd.

- **Rnd 1:** knit to last 3 sts of needle 1, ssk, k1, k20 (22) instep sts, with needle 3, k1, k2tog, knit to end.
- **Rnd 2:** knit.

Rep rnds 1 and 2 until 40 (44) stitches remain. Work even in Stockinette stitch until foot measures 4 (5) inches or desired length from back of heel.

Toe

- **Rnd 1:** on needle 1, knit to last 3 sts, ssk, k1; on needle 2, k1, k2tog, k to last 3 sts, ssk, k1; on needle 3, k1, k2tog, k to end.
- **Rnd 2:** knit.
- Rep rnds 1 and 2 until 10 (12) sts remain.

Larger Size Only

- Rep rnd 2 once more—10 (8) sts.

Finishing

- Slip the stitches from needle 3 to the right end of needle 1; you should have 5 (4) stitches on each needle.

- Graft the toe closed, or cinch up the toe like you might the top of a hat.

- Make a second sock. Weave in ends.

Christmas Stocking Knitting Pattern

Gauge

14 stitches and 7 rows to 4 inches in stockinette stitch on size 10 needles—this gives a firm fabric, less likely to stretch out of shape.

Size

Total length: 19 inches

Length from top to heel: 12 inches

Length from heel to toe: 10 inches

Width around: 12 inches

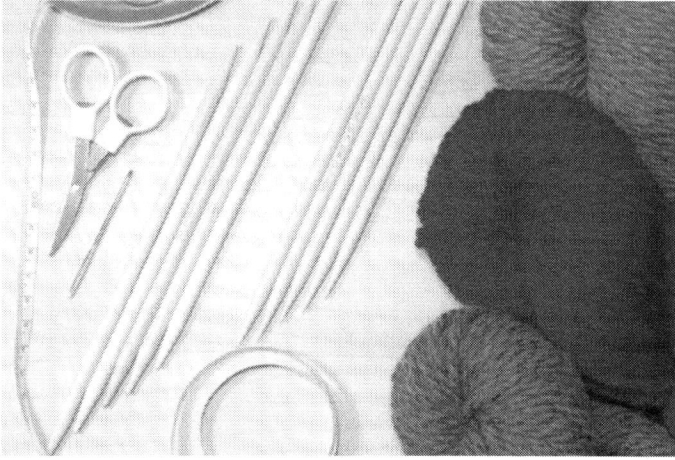

What you'll need:

Equipment/ Tools

- 1 Pair of size 10 US (6 mm) double-pointed needles

- 1 Pair of size 10.5 US (6.5 mm) double-pointed needles

- 1 Yarn needle

- 1 Tape measure

- 1 Pair of scissors

Materials

- 1 Skein of Cascade Yarns 128 Superwash in shade 900 charcoal, or about 80 yards of bulky weight yarn of your choice (color A)
- 1 Skein of Cascade Yarns 128 Superwash in shade 893 ruby, or about 80 yards of bulky weight yarn of your choice (color B)
- 1 Skein of Cascade Yarns 128 Superwash in shade 860 smoke heather, or about 80 yards of bulky weight yarn of your choice (color C)

Instructions

Knit the Cuff

- Cast on 40 stitches of Color B, spread out evenly across 4 size 10 double-pointed needles
- Join in the round
- Knit 12 rows in Stockinette
- Change to size 10.5 double-pointed needles
- Purl 1 row
- Knit 12 rows

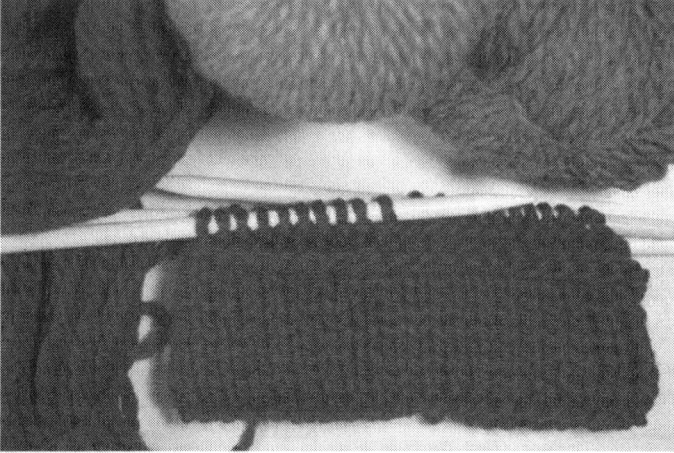

Make the Body of Stocking

The leg and foot of this stocking alternates between a solid stripe in color C and a patterned stripe with colors C and A.

- Change to C and work 5 rounds in stockinette stitch
- Change to A but do not cut the yarn for C
- Carrying both colors along the wrong side
- Work the following pattern in stockinette stitch
- Knit 1 round in A
- K3 in A, K1 in C, *K4 in A, K1 in C

- Repeat from * until 1 stitch remains

- K1 in A

- *K2 in A, K3 in C. Repeat from * to end

- K3 in A, K1 in C, *K4 in A, K1 in C

- Repeat from * until 1 stitch remains

- K1 in A

- Knit 1 round

Repeat these steps two additional times each. On the last row of the leg, only knit halfway.

Shape The Heel

The heel is worked on 20 stitches at the back of the stocking.

- Shape the heel using short row shaping along half of the round (20 stitches)
- Change to B and Knit to 1 stitch before the end of the round, wrap and turn
- Purl to 1 stitch before the end of the heel, wrap and turn
- Knit to 2 stitches before the end of the heel, wrap and turn
- Purl to 2 stitches before the end of the heel, wrap and turn

Continue in this manner until 7 stitches remain in the center between the wraps.

Increase Heel

- Knit to your first wrapped stitch

- Knit the wrap and the stitch together by picking up the wrapped stitch from front to back, wrap and turn

- Purl to your first wrapped stitch

- Purl the wrap and stitch together by picking up the wrapped stitch from back to front and placing it over and behind the stitch, wrap and turn

Repeat in this manner until you knit across the entire heel. Be sure to knit both wraps when you get to them.

Finish the Foot

Change to color C and return to the stripe pattern.

- Work 5 rounds in stockinette stitch

- Change to A but do not cut the yarn for C

Carrying both colors along the wrong side, work the following pattern in stockinette stitch.

- Knit 1 round in A

- K3 in A, K1 in C, *K4 in A, K1 in C

- Repeat from * until 1 stitch remains

- K1 in A

- *K2 in A, K3 in C

- Repeat from * to end

- K3 in A, K1 in C, *K4 in A, K1 in C

- Repeat from * until 1 stitch remains

- K1 in A

- Knit 1 row

- Repeat these steps once more.

Work the Toe

- Change to B and knit 1 round
- *SSK, K16, K2tog
- Repeat from * until end, knit 1 round
- *SSK, K14, K2tog
- Repeat from * until end, knit 1 round
- *SSK, K12, K2tog

- Repeat from * until end, knit 1 round

- *SSK, K10, K2tog

- Repeat from * until end, knit 1 round

- *SSK, K8, K2tog

- Repeat from * until end

Use the Kitchener stitch to connect the stitches on needles #1 and #2 to the stitches on needles #3 and #4.

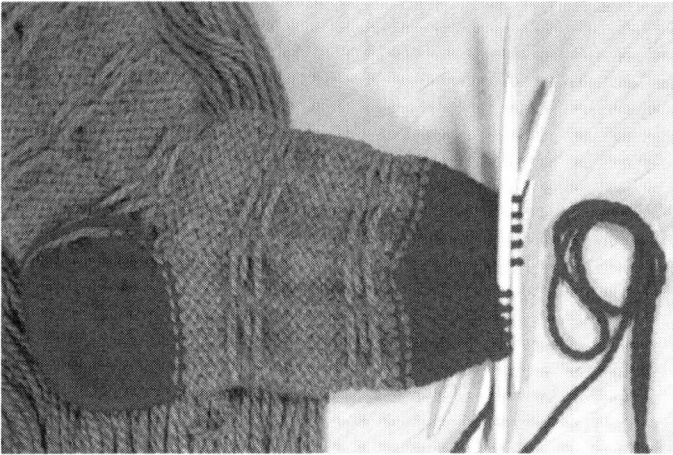

Complete the Finishing Touches

- Fold the cuff along the purled row toward the inside of the

stocking

- Sew from the wrong side

- Knit a three stitch i-cord (approximately 5-inches long)

- Bind off

- Shape into a loop and sew into the cuff

- Weave in all loose ends.

Knit Yoga Socks Pattern

Materials:

- Yarn in worsted or aran weight – your color choice is totally optional
- Knitting Needles, size 7 US
- Scissors
- Tapestry Needle

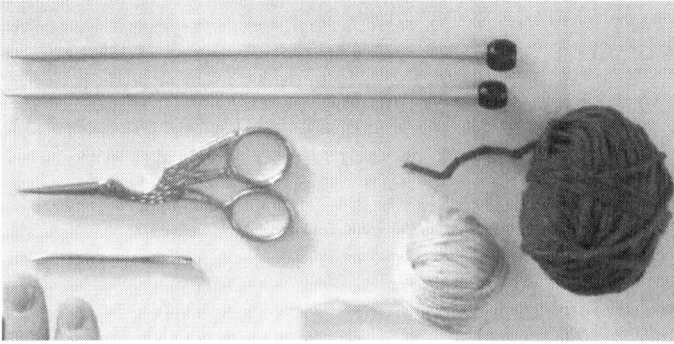

Instructions:

Cast On (36 Sts Small, 38 Sts Medium, 40 Sts Large, or 42 Sts XL)

Rows 1 – 6: Knit 1×1 Rib Stitch *K1, P1 *

Rows 7 – 16: Knit in Stockinette Pattern (Knit Right Side, Purl Wrong Side)

Row 17: Bind Off ½ of the stitches on your needle, then Knit the remaining stitches

Rows 1 - 6: *K1P1*

Rows 7 - 16: Stockinette Stitch

Row 17: BO 1/2, K 1/2

Row 18: P 1/2, Cable CO 1/2

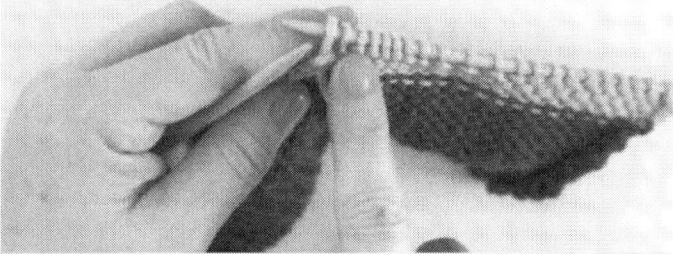

Rows 47 - 53: *K1, P1*

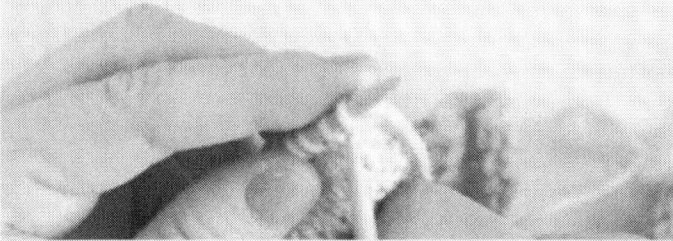

Rows 19 - 46: Stockinette Stitch

Row 18: Purl all stitches on your needle, then Cast On those stitches using the Cable Cast On Method to place the same number of stitches you originally cast on.

Rows 19 – 46 (or longer, if desired): Knit in Stockinette Pattern (Knit Right Side, Purl Wrong Side)

Rows 47 – 53 (last 6 rows): Knit 1×1 Rib Stitch *K1, P1 *

Finishing:

- **Stretchy Bind Off**
- **Seam up the edge**
- **Make Two and you are DONE!**

Printed in Great Britain
by Amazon